THE SPIRITS
NEED TO EAT

THE SPIRITS
NEED TO EAT

Francette Cerulli (signature)

—— *Poems by* ——
Francette Cerulli

Nine–Patch Press
Worcester, Vermont

The Spirits Need To Eat

Published by
Nine-Patch Press
579-B Minister Brook Road
Worcester, VT 05682

Printed in the United States

First Edition

Publisher's Cataloging in Publication Data

811.54
C   Cerulli, Francette, 1949-
         The spirits need to eat / poems by
        Francette Cerulli. — Worcester, VT :
        Nine-Patch Press, ©1999
        81 pages
        I. Title
ISBN: 0-9669473-0-4

Book design by Peter Holm, Sterling Hill Productions

ACKNOWLEDGMENTS

Big Fish: "The Rooms of Older Sisters"
Calliope (Roger Williams College): "The Bottle," "The
    Swimmer," "Second Fire: Going Back In," "Feeding
    the Second Fire"
Chester H. Jones Poetry Anthology: "The Spirits Need to Eat"
Cloverdale Review of Poetry & Criticism: "The Artisan"
Country Courier: "Birth Day," "Jealousy of Trees,"
    "Reliving History"
The Denny Poems: "Celia Going Under"
The Green Mountain Trading Post: "Baby Girl Found,"
    "Brushes," "Crazy Woman Hanging Out Clothes,"
    "Valentine for Zephyr, Age 12"
Kindling: Poems from Vermont Gatherings: "Grace,"
    "The Hunter," "Mother's Day Television"
Louisville Review: "Falling in Love with My Mother, Age 70"
Negative Capability: "The Black Skirt," "The Borrower,"
    "Kinds of Murder," "Dissection at Nine Years"
Vermont Life: "Civil War Photograph"
Vermont Woman: "Magazine Cover, December 1918"

I am grateful for the support of the Vermont Council on the
Arts for the year 1989-90 in the form of a Finalist Award
for Poetry.

    For being in on the ground floor and sticking with me, I
thank my mother, Mary Genevieve Buck and my father,
Nicholas Francis Cerulli.

    I am deeply grateful to Mark Doty and Wally Roberts for a
car ride on a dark and rainy night that helped me think I
might be a writer.

    For their love, artistry and inspiration, I thank Beth

Adams, Helen Butterfield, Tami Calliope, Judy Chalmer, Rickey Gard Diamond, Nadell Fishman, Jody Gladding, Janet Hewitt, Gary Moore, Sherry Olson, Jonathan Sa'adah, Diane Swan, Ezra Tishman, and my pen pal Jo Ann Hatstat.

For bracing me for and sheltering me from life's storms I thank my dear friends Deborah Bogart, Lynn Heglund, Catherine Jay, Linda Leehman, Terry Padilla, Jonathan Parke, and Suzanne Rhodes.

For encouragement at crucial times I thank Toni-Lee Capossela, Mark and Kurt Cerulli, Martha Christina, Doug Currier, Michael Moore, Lynn Cerulli Phillips, and Susan Walp.

I thank my children: Tovar Cerulli, for his encouragement, generosity, and steadfast love; Celia Cerulli Pashe, for her irrepressibility and edible poetry; and Zephyr Cerulli Billingsley, for her tender heart and the supreme gift of crying at my readings. For the especially sweet rewards of being a wicked little stepmother, I thank my beautiful bonus daughter, Etta Meyers Eckart.

Mick Eckart, my husband, is proof that the best sometimes gets saved for last. I thank him for warming and caring for me body and soul, and for the prod and comfort of his humor, by-product of a dangerously metaphorical mind.

And for all of you who asked for my book, here, at last, is your answer, with my heartfelt thanks for your long encouragement.

For my brothers and sisters—
Toni-Lee, Mark, Lynn, and Kurt

and for my children—
Tovar, Celia, Zephyr, and Etta

CONTENTS

THE SPIRITS
NEED TO EAT

RELIVING HISTORY

Son in Mourning

The priest chews gum and says words
over my mother that are supposed to
sound like grief. I look at him in wonder.
He is somewhere else. He is not even trying
to step into my skin for a moment.

He didn't even ask for the stories.
If he did I would have told him how she
wore a hat with a blue feather,
the same blue as that dress,
how she sat on a stool to do the ironing.

If he had asked
I would have told him
how we loved to pick her up
and carry her around
when we finally got big.

But I would not tell him
about the bread dough,
how when she was done kneading it
and it was resting on the table
she would let me cup my hand over it
just for a minute. The little mound
of dough was warm and softly blistering
and I was starting to wonder about girls

and just as I was about to keel over
from pleasure this woman my mother
would laugh and give me a whack on the rump
and tell me to go out and play.

I would maybe, maybe, tell him

about the dress and maybe the hat
with the blue feather

but no, not even that, because
now as I look at him in wonder
and watch him saying those words
that don't touch skin

I want to scream at him,
Don't you know we live by the word?
Don't you know that words leave one body to enter another?
That the word "hot" makes us jump,
"stubbed" makes our big toe hurt,
and when we hear "cut"
we smell disinfectant?

So I sit here not believing it.
I watch in wonder as he flings words
out of his mouth without loving them first.
Amazed, I watch the words jump out of his blood in terror,
loud and dry and not one of them
the one I've been waiting for.

I turn away in wonder
and start to listen for one quiet word.

Soak it patiently for months
in this roar of sad blood.

I heft it in my hand,
bring it to my mouth,
taste comfort and salt.

Churching
(for the priests of St. Al's)

You priests, all of you sons, say a woman must be
cleansed after childbirth, she must kneel down
two steps below you in the church, be sprinkled
with holy water to wash away her defilement.

But you don't fool any mothers with your
little ceremony. They all know you're messing
in your vestments you're so scared of what They can do.
How They can have those big living things come out
of Them over and over and still live. How They can
bleed month after month, enough blood for a serious wound,
and still talk normally and walk around.

Those women you stand there saying pure words
over, pretending to make presentable to God—

They are your mother. They are the mother of God.
Before God even thought about you Their milk
was in His mouth. Their blood is the blood
that covered you before you made a sound.
Their blood is the holy blood that made you.

Apologia of the Kindling-Gatherers
(for Janet Lind Hewitt)

We don't know how or when it was born,
this constant nipping itch
to pick up sticks, pinecones,
anything small enough to catch fire
quickly and burn in the dark.

Maybe when mornings began to bite,
the need came on us then, to see
kindling around us, mounded
in baskets, piled in boxes nearby
where we could touch it often,
all the empty cups in our houses filled.

Remember it starting as a game?
We mimed our solid-seeming elders
(those warm talking walls
stood between us and our winters).
Then, with every cold season,
the comings and goings of lovers,

our pretending tapped the bone and was real.
Now an urge strong as decorum
genuflects us, we gather the same small objects
again and again without being bored.
For with each small wood we harvest,
in the reaching down of the arm,

the plucking of the fingers,
we hope for warmth and remember
its lack. No trees topple for us,
no wood piles up in the shed.

For our work is small,
only noticed when it's missing,
that necessary middle flame
between the spark and the bankable fire.

Civil War Photograph

This will be a long exposure,
the photographer says.
So the soldiers have stopped chewing
their tobacco. They don't want their women
to see them with their faces all mushy,
or with three eyes.
They let their muscles settle into
the tiredness underneath.
The photographer has placed them
carefully in the shade for the assault,
so the sunlight will not draw irreverent
lines all over their serious bodies,
or make them squint.

They sit on the photographer's chairs
pretending to look eternal, holding
their tired hands still on their legs.
They don't tap a foot or blink.
Their eyes water.

Over them, one small tree blows
back and forth in the breeze.
It makes a smeared
black-and-white umbrella
behind them. It says to us:
in this place, time passed.

Reliving History

This must have been what it was like
the summer before the Great War,
quiet towns just like this, men and women
riding their bicycles through the streets
after dinner, no sound except their pedaling
and the squeaking of their seats under them,

the wet metal sound of grass being cut
always behind houses, out of sight,
all human voices murmuring or far away,
the pink and red zinnias blazing out at them
in that moment before dark,
the mix of the first woodsmoke
and the last apples so sharp
and sweet you could weep.

Magazine Cover, December 1918*

Santa was supposed to have left an hour ago.
His wife reminds him of the time,
but without conviction. So many boys
have dropped off the list, you see.
He cannot even pretend to be jolly.

His cheeks are pale and his eyes cannot
see far. He has been sitting in the same chair
at his workbench for the past half hour,
twirling the propeller
of a beautiful toy warplane.

In his lap is a beautiful toy soldier,
a beautiful toy tank, and a troop carrier
any boy would be proud to own.

He is thinking of his sons, his grandsons,
that sweet flesh he will never kiss again,
that sweet flesh that will end when he does.

*Front Cover, *Pictorial Review*, December 1918. World War One ended in
November, 1918. Over 8 million died.

Grace

We must not turn on the lights in our houses
until the sun has been down for one hour.

We must sit here at the window, or there
on the porch, or just around the kitchen table,

wherever it catches us,
and watch it leave.

We must remember the time when
we had nothing against the dark.

We must remember the easy grace
of letting darkness fall.

THE MISSING

The Bottle

Back when my father was so small
he was barely walking,
he once tripped and fell on a broken bottle.
Back then he did not lie there screaming.
Back then he was still determined.
He got up and walked to his mother,
who was talking to a friend in her world
way up there, and yelled,
Mama, Mama, held onto her leg and
pulled on her skirt over and over until
she looked down and saw the blood
pumping out of his neck.

Without a thought she picked him up,
clapped him to her breast, stuck her
finger in the bloody hole, and ran
a mile to the doctor without stopping.

Later, when he grew to be a man,
he loved to tell this story to his children,
of how his mother saved his life, and we could
still see, without being too obvious about
looking, the white scar on his neck.

And later, when he surrounded himself with
a wife and five children all looking
at him to keep them alive, he fell
on some bottle or other every night
until he could barely walk again,
clutching at the clothes of his wife
and the leg of his daughter as he went down
into that baby place again,
waiting for someone who would pick him up and
carry him the whole distance just for love.

The Artisan

One night when I was still small enough
to hide under the buffet and eat stolen butter,
we were clearing the supper table between
dinner and dessert. I watched my father walk

down the short hall to the bathroom.
His leather slippers scuffed on the tiles
he'd set into the floor himself. The tiles
had come on a strong net backing. He'd laid

them precisely onto the floor, then smeared
in the grout with his thumb. Grout is something
that you put in place and it stays there.
As I watched him walk, he slowly fell

into the wall on his right. This falling,
the two martinis every night—
My father didn't stagger.
It was the world.

Poems in the Mail from My Father

Now that they've opened you up once
and the heart attacked you anyway,
now that you know
we're really going to lose,
you send me the pieces of yourself
you've kept in a box for,
let's say, fifty years.

Now that you know we're really
going to lose that
long chosen silence,
you let these papers flutter through
the mail in twos and threes,
giving me the boy and then
the young man I never knew,
letting me see you as my mother saw you
before you both knuckled under
and turned each other into saddles,
then hung five children
around the edges like fringe.

And I cry at every one to see
you showing yourself off
for the very first time again.

Mothers to Our Own Father

We are the daughters who were taught to be mothers
to our own father. During those three sweet days
of our infancy, we learned to be comforters without comfort,
anchors without anchorage, all the while perfecting the art
of seeming large and heavy with wisdom.

We may use ourselves up
before we remember stupidly the one thing
that got missed, that skipped step
of being some man's daughter.

Our father may die out on the ocean, happy even,
before we remember to ask him for something,
anything, as daughters need to do.

He may give us gifts of money, or a two-minute rest
on the chest of an old bird so strained with the effort of love
we're afraid we'll break him with our own muscular sorrow.

So like most mothers of difficult children,
we don't keep track of what we've given this one.

We look for his missing parts in our lovers,
cry like one-year-olds at his final going,
and feel a mysterious tiredness when he is gone.

The Genius

(for Debbye Sessions, in memoriam)

In a world this small we hear things:
how considerately you left, and the note
apologizing for missing that meeting.

I knew you during that slot of time
when we were all making babies,
learning the scientific names for openings
and emergences, squeezing out those
wet curled buds who'd suddenly run out of room
and couldn't live in there any more.

In a world this big we miss things,
how the last time I saw you you tried to tell me
how it was when you were small and the men you trusted
kept squeezing themselves into your small body,
how there was no room for them
and you couldn't run out of the room.

And you, nimble genius of survival, turned yourself
instead into a whole houseful of friends
who later wouldn't leave you alone,
couldn't even let you decide whether or not
to have a cup of coffee,
but kept arguing among themselves,
hanging around behind doors
in case you needed them again,
their bickering voices and desires
pushing and pulling at your one mere body.

In a world this full we expect things,
how the right words will show up for the occasion
so we can type a neat page, take it to the service

or mail it to the family, hoping to help us all
in the letting you go and in the keeping.

But nothing, not even planting the garden
or firming the dirt around the various roots,
nothing would do it that summer,
until the very end of the season
a house burned in town,
driving the family out.

That is when you left me.
How long I stood and watched for you,
you couldn't come to the windows.

The Remnant
(for Kurt)

It never occurred to me until now
what it must have been like for you,
the last one left in that house with them.
Paralyzing dinners at that huge round table,
symbol of completion, our father in his
hot distracted despair coming up on fifty,
wondering how the hell he would ever make
something of himself. Our mother sitting
straight, serving you, her spine and jaw
wired together with the stale rage you were
born into, waiting for you to leave just so
she could. How strange, to have your one
parent's eyes looking inward to himself,
always stopping before they reached you,
the other's always looking beyond you to
something so much louder. And their own
wistful son, folding down his own pink ear
for comfort, trying, perhaps, to create
the sounds of a small, distant sea.

When you visited me back then, you grabbed
onto me like a little monkey whenever I
got close enough. And I, who had a lover
at the time, looked past you to him as I
peeled you from my arm like a glove.
Seeing everything through the simple-minded eyes
of sex, I was afraid you wanted to be my lover.
I didn't have the sense to see you were just
going for the softest thing in the cage.

Was that when you started saying,
I have no use for you, and put on the

heavy black robes of the judge?

Last night I dreamed we were married. Your
shiny black robe opened to show a godlike chest,
and an arrow with oiled black feathers protruding
from your right breast. There was no blood.
You said, *Oh, that just stays there.*
You bought me a magenta tea gown.
There was never any question of sex.

Now, at thirty, you've spread a whole feast out
around you. Your wife and daughter look straight
into your eyes. They ask you questions. The jaws
of the starving little monkey are beginning
to open, his eyes to focus on the food. His mouth
begins to taste the goodness of his life.

Thanksgiving Requiem

With all due respect I want to thank you,
my son's father in heaven, for dying when you did.

Not for your death, over which I cried louder
than anyone. But for this gift, this boy,
over whose heart you threw the finest grey veil
when I let you have him seven years ago.

Unseeable as water, strong as fear,
it kept him from stepping too far from you,
too close to me, even for visits.

Every week now I get to see him, to touch his skin,
to feed him, even to stack his firewood.
We laugh at each other now and swap life stories.

You may say I sound like his house servant.
And it's true. I'm not displeased with the job.
He would never show any servant what he shows me.

He left his shirt off once after a shower.
Showing me his body like a surprise
he'd been saving for years, he said, Look at this,
the way these muscles do this practically all by themselves.

And as he flexed just a little bit, not so much as to be unseemly,
I saw how each muscle tended to separate cleanly
from the others, connecting to bone and its neighbors
only by the finest elastic wires under the thinnest of skins.

I only hesitated for a second. Stripping off
my outer shirt and flexing my arm like a
magazine ad for athletic equipment, I said,

See that? Your grampa has muscles like that.
I got them from him and you got them from me.
And that skin, too, that slides on you
like a cat's? That's mine, too.

THE MOTHERS

Baby Girl Found

He found her wrapped in a brown towel
beside the highway department dumpster.
She was so cold she was blue, so new
her umbilical stump still drooped softly
from her belly like the limp stem
of some fantastic fruit.

He picked her up in his huge gloved
highway department hands and
carried her to his truck. Inside the cab
he turned on the light, peeled the damp towel
from her body and held her
under the blast of the truck heater.

Giant midwife bent over her in the frozen morning,
he watched for the smallest sign.
It was her second birth.

Mother's Day Television

I walk home after a day in the town.
But I find my town is not just this town.

My town is now Nicaragua, and the pattern of winter salt
drying on my driveway turns to the blood
of Nicaragua's children, as I watch.

My town is now El Salvador, and its mothers
walk up my steps and die on my porch, as I watch.

My town is now Cambodia, and the skulls of its fathers
surface in the dishwater in my kitchen sink, as I watch.

The nightly news flattens the globe in a second,
and I feel my back pressed up against the pointed spine
of the starving Ethiopian woman whose child, the caption says,
died the next day before the newspaper hit the porch.

We two mothers could easily exchange souls at that moment,
across the bridge of our bones, and I could be in her body,
too weak even to mourn, while she is in my body,
and walks out of my kitchen, down my porch steps,
and out my driveway.

On the street, she and my neighbors would spend money,
pretending to buy used clothes from each other,
and send it all to me,
so I, in her body, could eat.

Feeding the Second Fire

When fire comes secretly into our house, the town says,
We can't imagine it, how it must feel.
We say, Yes, it was quite a shock.
We don't say the truth, that we can't imagine it either,
that our imaginations have failed us here,
that we are afraid we will never imagine anything again.

But as we walk by the doors of our new rooms,
rooms so new they don't even smell like us yet,
we see her out of the corners of our eyes.
She is a small girl with tangled hair,
sitting in the middle of our bed.
Her skin is tired and dry, her hair, airy as wood shavings.

She has wrapped herself up to the neck in our bedsheets,
lonely little mountain, a science project volcano
waiting for the heat to build up.

We feed her ice cream and buttered toast,
talking to her in short quiet words:
puddle, map, little sip.

Making no sudden movements,
we unswaddle her turn by turn,
walking around her in measured steps.
Uncovered, her tiny body heats the house.

We unbutton our bellies and show her that we, too,
have small fires inside us.

We feed her blue roses and cool water.
And when we stroke her hair gently with our careful hands,
it does not ignite.

Slowly we get close enough to whisper.
We murmur in her ear,
Come, live with us, little one. You shall be our third daughter.

The Blind

The blind mother walks down the street in winter,
her child and her seeing-eye dog both on leashes.
The dog leads the woman and the woman leads the child.
The child trips on a piece of ice and falls. She rolls over slowly
in her snowsuit and waits on the sidewalk,
looking up at the sky, waiting for her mother quietly.

As soon as her mother feels the pull on the line,
she stops. As soon as the dog feels the pull on the line,
she stops and waits. Even when the mother lets go
of the dog's leash to help her child, the dog stands and waits.
The mother lifts the child slowly by the arm
and sets her on her feet. Holding her child's hand in one hand
and the dog's leash in the other, she continues on her way.

Everyone, even her children, can see
they must wait for her at times. Those are her rules.
I envy her her dog, her child that patiently waits
and screams less than other children, her walking stick
that she uses when the kids are at home with their father
and she wants to get somewhere fast.

I want to have my faults in some easily recognizable form,
detachable letters that I could put on my coat for advertising.
A would be for anger, *I*, for inadequate today.
I would keep my stick by the door and use it on those days,
poke that red tip out in front of me like a flare.
It would say to my husband, my children,
Look, I have these wounds, but I can take care of you
if you just make allowances.

My Mother's Hands

Doing this automatic thing called breadmaking,
I see my hands as if my daughter is watching.

Your hands are so careful, she says enviously,
whenever she sees me sewing or making bread,
bringing something out of nothing
with no mistakes that she can see.

Your hands are so careful, she says with wonder,
as if my hands are two pets that I keep on
a leash and have taught to be gentler than I am.

And I can see now that doing these things,
my hands are my mother's, the knuckles
growing thick, the crinkling skin thin and fine
as onionskin, the blue veins large
with dedication to the task.

I want to tell my girl that making something perfectly
will not guarantee her happiness,
but she has the fierce passion of the flagellant
whenever she makes a mistake,
so I don't talk about her.
I just say, like my mother did,
try it again until you get it right.

And after she goes to sleep I look
in the mirror and repeat the lesson.

Cleaning House
(for Zephyr)

I don't understand how they can fly,
those sluggish metal boxes with wings stuck on.

Yesterday she left in one as I watched
willing the lazy thing up,
not really believing it would work,
needing to see it go up if it could,
needing to see it go down if it did,
needing to hold her in my eyes no matter what.

This was just a practice hop.

Today I clean house,
suck up dust with my shining wand
so the the red tile floors can show true.

I brush the new blue rugs,
drag the dulling lint towards me,
and the color comes up.

I will brush her hair often
between now and her next flight,
burnish the red-brown in that heavy shining mop,
pull those dark strands towards me
until the last particle
of drag-causing dust is gone.

Falling in Love with My Mother, Age 70

i

Folded small in the translucent envelopes of our mothers'
bodies, we first learned the steps of ballroom dancing.
Like old village stories they entered us.
We began that long discipline of the cells.

In the filtered red light, the muffled music
and watered voices, we learned the art of sliding
easily into spaces left empty by others,
believing that is where we most want to be.

The man leads, we were told. When he moves
towards us, we step back. When he moves back
we step happily again into that empty place
he's left. And after all, isn't this dancing?

Yes, say our grandmothers, *it is, of a sort.*
I guess, say our daughters, as their eyes shift
sideways, looking for a danceable tune.

ii

Then once, at a wedding, it happens.
When our men are otherwise occupied
we glide into the lull.

Starting out with a straight cha-cha,
we do it the old way first,
holding hands, pretending I'm the man.

Then we let each other go

34

Our husbands, our children fall away
as we embroider carelessly, the space
between us becoming so large
we scare each other, then so small
we almost collide.

We play around with those same old steps
till we get something new
until we get that wide
open blue of your eyes
that just-before-flying
just-before-falling smile
wide open sea of your eyes.

THE FAIRY TALES

Transubstantiation

Do you like these flowers?
I made them myself.
Panic was the magic seed
taken in springtime
with tears swallowed down
into the uterus.

A miracle better than the loaves and fishes
that my poor culture grew in such a tiny rain-barrel
three times, almost four,
into creatures colored like anemones,
walk-about, phosphorescent.

Pinocchio's Mother

(for Mary Azarian)

What do you say to her,
that woman who comes to you
in those last few moments of sleep?

She holds up a chisel
and a block of wood.

Then she tells you
you're going to have a baby,
and she knows what she's talking about.

Her squared hands are covered
with tiny crescent-shaped scars
from small slips of the knife.

And even though you wake yourself up
saying *no*, that flat word bounces off
the dumb wooden ceiling above you,

It bounces off the morning air,
it has already lodged inside you,
a small moon.

The Black Skirt

(for Celia)

Lorca's in the woodpile.
He wants my daughter for his own.
Every night I pile the logs onto him,
and every night he almost breaks out,
almost gets the chance to see her dancing.

She's letting me know now she thinks
my methods are crude. Her eyes as she twirls
smile at me. Her eyes are shining spears,
sly and pleased, seeing everything,
and pleased. But my methods are crude.

Watch this, the corners of her eyes say.
And as she twirls faster the black satin skirt
we made together rises higher and higher,
showing me and Lorca and the moon
more and more long leg and then
the pale yellow satin covering up
what Lorca thinks he wants most.

She twirls out the shining black lake around
her waist and ripples and waves it for her own
pleasure. She is going fast enough now to
cut down small trees if she feels like it.

Lorca is quiet beside me. We both see
she will not be forced to a yes or a no.
We both see that someday she will twirl
slowly enough to invite someone in.

Celia Going Under

Sixteen, her hair and skin the color of cornsilk,
she lies on the couch in the dark like
some failing goddess of the crops.
This is too much like the old myths—

her father died less than a year ago,
her brother lives far away, and her stepfather
has been too long across the ocean.
All the young men who love her

just happen to be on their way out of town.
When she walks down the street
the sidewalk shakes with the heavy
rooted joy of her feet, and her dancing

is like the sun playing with its own storms.
But every so often it gets to her,
these men constantly leaving.
I want her to tell me these things,

but she is her own woman now, and
guards her suffering from me like the
irreplaceable seeds of her own future.
In the kitchen, I make spaghetti sauce

like a good mama, for just the two of us.
I chop onions as if her life depends on it.
I peel the smooth white pills of garlic.

In the Woods

One morning you ride away from your house,
you ride away slowly on a strong brown horse
straight out of a fairy tale,
away from your sweet husband or wife,
down the dirt road through the grey trees.

You think you're on your way to town.
But before you get very far what do you think?
You see a young man waiting on the side of the road,
straight as a tree, tough as the woods,
not even leaning on anything. He rolls his eyes
nervously from side to side, trying to pretend
he just happens to be standing there in the wilderness,
that he has better things to do.

He is the most beautiful, tough, brainless human being
you've ever seen in your life, and you want him so much
that he becomes an axis, the trees start to rotate
slowly around him as you almost ride by.

Then you can't help yourself he's part of you already
it would be a lie not to, so you lean down as you pass
and you kiss him you feel like you're turning inside out
and he kisses you back this is what he was waiting for and
you know you can't have him, and it is so unbearably sweet
and full of that longing that you only feel when you know
it could never work but you feel it anyway.
Then you gather this longing into your hands.
Cup it there under your ribs like a new pregnancy
until it takes on a form of its own.
Put it carefully in your coat pocket.
And after your errands, when you get home,
you carry it quietly into your house

43

and slide it between the bedsheets
of the one you married long ago.

You slide it a little more than halfway down
and leave it there for later, this warm heavy gift
that came to you one morning when you rode away.

Kinds of Murder
(for Tovar)

Walking to the market for milk,
I question my son casually
about the Persian fairy tale.
He liked it okay, he says.

Speaking from this cool New England hill
in summer, instructing my young son, I shudder
properly and remind him of all the violence there,
of Morgiana pouring hot oil onto the forty thieves,
blistering them to death one by one as they slept
in their man-sized oiljars awaiting dawn.

But she had to do that, he says.
There weren't any police back then.

I can see he's back there without me now, roaming
through the baked alleys in the stinking heat,
smelling sugared almonds, curry, honeyed seedcakes.

Pertinent facts start coming back to me:
that Ali Baba bought the girl in the marketplace,
that her beauty would have made her a prostitute
except for this man, who made her his daughter
and loved her in that way only.
That they were both lucky and they knew it.
That the money for her freedom did indeed come
from the thieves' cave and without their permission,
but it was also their habit to cut people into bits
for taking just one piece of gold, then
string the flesh up to dry in the hot wind.

I think of forty men with swords sleeping
in my little back yard in metal oildrums overnight

(the lids slightly tilted for breathing), waiting
to hack us apart in the cool Vermont morning.
They are dreaming of mistakes my father made years ago.

The authorities would never believe me.

Stumbling, I check my supply of cooking oil,
line up my largest pots on the counter.

THE CHILDREN

The Swimmer
(for Zephyr)

At the community pool my daughter says
open your legs (who else would I take such
instructions from?) *so I can swim through them.*
I brace myself for the shock. I'm sure her hard noggin
will ram my crotch, but she is learning fast this year,
she goes deep enough and slides through easily, front to back.

Stay there, she says, *I'm coming back through.*
I look down and see her head emerge first,
then without a pause her gold body in a turquoise suit
the same color as the surrounding water.

As her legs and feet shoot through, my body forms a prayer
over her, that her life will be like this, lightly bumping
the sides, causing little harm, finding other swimmers
to nudge up against and sweetly touch undersides.

Lynn's Middle Name

(for Lynn Beatrice Cerulli)

Whenever you said your middle name,
 you spat it out like a bad taste: *Beet-triss-I-hate it!*
as if someone had just yanked the red root
out of the ground still covered with clumps of dirt
and was trying to make you eat it like that.

We didn't know then how like a song your name was
when said correctly, the way Dante said it to his love,
a four-syllabled Italian canto,
Bay-a-tree-chay, Bay-a-tree-chay,
a word small boys with plump brown legs might sing
over and over, once on the out-breath, once on the in–
as they ran about their business: Bay-a-tree-chay, Bay-a-tree-chay,
just for the mouth pleasure of shaping it.

Now when I slice beets for the table,
I hear your complaint as I marvel at their beauty.
The pink concentric circles in the purple-red flesh
are the rising steps of Purgatory, then curved stairs up to Heaven,
where both you Beatrices gaze down on us through eyes of sky.

Look into this bowl, how shining beautiful
these several red medallions.
How did you land here among us?

Valentine for Zephyr, Age 12

The night before valentines are due,
I take you to the movie about Vincent
whose paintings you love. Too late
I realize it's a mistake. You knew about his ear
and you know the definition of prostitute,
but neither one of us was ready
to see him cut himself until he bled,
see him in the brothel
with his rotten teeth and his real women.

On the way home in the starry night we hold hands,
wonder what his parents must have been like,
what cruelty may have happened to him,
and you show me the belt of Orion,
clean and shining and always in place.

Remember this forever, then:
I cannot imagine not loving you,
even when this body is gone.

So if I ever die, look up into the dark
and find me hundreds of times there,
each place you can faintly imagine a line
tracing the shape of a valentine.

Garden

The leggy tomatoes, just starting to form
their small green marbles, lean on the fibrous gladiolas
like adolescent girls often love to lean on their mothers,
with twice their actual weight.

Now, when the tomatoes are so young
they're still dusted with a sheen of golden hairs,
they prop their chins, their hands, their elbows
on the slender fronds of the gladiola and hang there,
nuzzling, waiting for an answer, or advice.

Full of the rising push of love,
they suspend themselves from their mothers
like heavy necklaces, fiercely moaning:
How do I do this, Mother?
Will you know me if I finish this thing?

The Borrower

She appropriates clothes as only a
teenage girl can. How can I say no
to someone who wears everything so well?

All my clothes want to go to her. Hanging
in my closet, they agitate softly. Lying
in the dark in my dresser drawers, they

start to unfold. *We would look so much
better on a younger woman*, they whisper.
Let us go. The day after her father dies,

she puts on his old jeans without asking
a soul. She rolls them three times at the
waist so they won't fall off. They make her

look fat. Wearing her dead father, she could
give a shit. Next she goes for his Pierre Cardin
robe, says she likes the little monogram.

I find it wrapped around her bedpillow,
complete with belt, as if she could turn
her pillow into her father's chest, equipped

with warmth and a heartbeat, just by covering it
with his clothing. For many nights she sleeps
like this. Till the day she tells me, laughing,

that she woke with his belt across her forehead,
like some paternal claim. I make her remove the
belt. I look into her eyes, the golden blue,
the eyes of her father. I say to him inside her,
This garment you may not take.

Birth Day

Fourteen years ago he slid from me,
a squeaking little thing—
a boy. He needed pushing and pulling
to make him uncurl and brave the light.

Again I see it's all happening too fast for him.
His arm and leg bones lengthening by the day,
his shoulders giant coat-hangers
barely disguised in skin and muscle.

His new body keeps trying to curl up
on him, go out of alignment,
until he despairs and asks me
how to stand up straight.

I tell him to pretend there is a string
coming out of the top of his head,
holding it up, and that everything else
will just fall into line.

He tries it and laughs.
He anticipates that every once in awhile
the string will pull a little too tight
and he will be walking in the air.

Son at Seventeen

My son, an expert by overexposure,
recognizes the song before I do,
the best one of the year
about how sex is good for everybody.

This large man who was a boy a year ago
cranks up the radio till the car
is a bulging capsule of sound,
heavy on the bass.

As he drives, he sings every word loudly,
with cellular belief.
He will have it all, give it all
in his time, probably soon.

My heart begins to vibrate dangerously
at the lowest frequencies.
Tonight I feel old enough to be mother to a man.

I mime my fear to him,
my hand on my chest, my eyes wide.
I can feel it in my chest, I scream.

He stops singing long enough to nod,
delighted that I have noticed.
It gets better, he yells.

MARRYING

The Spirits Need to Eat
(for Avery)

> "The time comes when you have no food except that
> which has been dedicated for you to eat, and there is
> no certainty of friends."
> —Tibetan Book of the Dead

It's been half a year since you flew out forever,
fourteen since we shared a house, or a bed.
I've tried everything to help you on your long grey way:
wishing you well, wishing I'd known my own strength
back then so I could've treated you to the surplus.
I've even been reading you an old poem from Tibet
to make your journey safe and help you to enlightenment.
And all the time I scurry around, a clucking hen
with eggs in two nests, checking on our two children,
making sure we all know there's one of us left down here.

Nothing quite did it for me, though, until last week,
when our son asked me to bake him some cookies.
He turns eighteen tomorrow.
I ate myself into a bellyache,
then remembered you out there in the dark.
So I zipped two of them inside the front of my jacket
(chocolate loses its flavor when chilled),
and took them out to you. On the rough airstrip
you cleared, the one you'll never land on,
I called you: *Hey, I brought you some cookies.*
You want some?

I left them in the open, on a white rock,
so you could find them easily.

Icarus Had a Son

(for Catherine Jay)

To Icarus, our love was a pleasant fling,
nice practice run for the big one.
But it brought us our boy,

light and springy as balsa,
so blond and bright
even that man got broody.

As father he still stayed bird, while I,
brought to ground by the milky weight of feeding,
couldn't climb a tree without getting woozy.

After the crash one day I slipped,
mentioned his father the eagle, tethered
my tongue too late, then kept a sharp eye.

I watched him start spending nights
in the woods, stride out mornings
his fists full of feathers.

He learned to carve bird-shapes,
wing-shapes, of wood.
Curled shavings pile around him like down.

Now he wants to marry a sweet little jay,
the kind that nests in houses and prefers to walk.
I try to hide my high delight,

say *Fine fine, what food can I bring?*
think *Marry a bird,*
you won't be one.

Second Fire: Going Back In

With spring, things are coming undone.
Frozen water from the firefighters' hoses that has glued
this house together for the last ten weeks is melting today.
This is the last day to look for things.
I find a steel pendulum, a brass buckle, a penny, a quarter.
Soon we'll knock the place down and start over.

Outside, the first sap is running, while on the doorframe
of what used to be the bathroom, a long narrow delta
of thick water bleeds down the smoked woodwork
to the floor. Open to the waves of cold and warmth now,
the wood in this house finally has an excuse to remember
what it felt like to be a tree in spring.

And I am no longer amazed that this house built of trees
burned so fast and hot and took so much with it,
but that it held itself still for so long,
resisting the memory of what it was.

For all those hundred years it got drier and drier.
The water left it, and the memory of trees got sharper
and more rasping until the house began to heave
and remember the up and down of the sap
that was no longer there. It tried to cry but
there wasn't even enough water in its cells for a tear.
It said to itself, *Trust me trust me*
I won't let anything happen to you,
like any lover to any hot virgin.
Let's just remember once more.
And at that moment it started the trip back.

Letter from Penelope

When you sailed off to fight almost twenty years ago
I never imagined this limbo; only victory or death.
And as the survivors trickled home they told me nothing sure,
just rumor after rumor of goddesses wanting you.

You're not the only one who's wanted.
Though only mortals, the men here
have been at me for years, their eyes bulging for riches,
their tunics for something else.

With you away, I took on your wiles.
Five years ago I thought up the story of the loom.
Your father's shroud is almost done, a clever joke—
I doubt he'll ever die.

But now at night when I pick the threads back out,
it's not to put off my suitors,
though it's not that they're not worth avoiding.
Slitting and gutting our once-great herds,
they're an army of looters just strutting as lovers.

But I have bigger things to think on.
There's something moving in the shroud.
Things I can see. With eyes. They look at me,
seeing not a collection of virtues, a full bag of money,
or a king's widow with a string of fat cattle attached.

They alone will finally bed me.
They know who I am.

Lewis and Clark

(for Mick)

The timing of this whole expedition took me by surprise—
no packing, no planning, I didn't even leave my house
before the damn thing was underway
and I was migrating fast from that place of cruelty,
that town back there I'm learning to call Old Hat.

I can't even say I've dreamed of this.
Though I did see your face once in my sleep,
I had no idea of the geography here,
how sometimes behind a big rock or a tree
I'd find these gifts of food on the ground and recognize them
as ones I'd offered again and again somewhere else,
always to men with long lists of allergies.

Strange,

that in the photos I send back from this fat place
my friends say my face looks lighter,

that here where there is so much
nothing gets wasted or thrown away,

how I have moved with you
into this country of unimagined kindness.

Cherry Trees
(for Mick)

There's no fancy way to say this.
The two cherry trees down the street remind me of us.

Their trunks are so spiraled that years ago they must have
come twirling up out of the ground like barber poles,
crazy with life like we were before we had to stop
and think about happiness.

We stand here now loaded with lessons repeated so often
they're turning sweet,
we're introducing ourselves to each other
with something like accuracy,
> *I do these things sometimes,*
> *can you live with it?*

And somehow the answer keeps coming up yes,
it must have been last summer's growth,
that last little twist that brought us face to face.

The Couple

She dives into her dreams wearing goggles
and a long breathing-hose,
picks up sand-dollars there,
feels their weight.

He lets his dreams sidle up to him,
rub along his side while he sniffs the air
for incoming weather systems,
or cradles the head of his horse in his lap
instead of eating lunch.

He rearranges his house for her,
she rearranges her dreams,
they overlap for days,
even hours at a time,

then separate. She rides out on his horse for entire nights
while he sleeps, her dreams breathing beside him,
holding her place in the bed.

GRACE

Jealousy of Trees

A tree in February has no needs.
A woman has plenty.
The tree stands still as iron,
and as thick. Leaves, fruit and seeds
are in her. She is so stuffed
with the raw material of her own
promise, she has no room for jealousy
of what she will be next month,
next year.

If I walk fast and hard for three blocks,
then stand very still and forget everything,
I should become the tree, waiting.

The Hunter
(for Mark)

I have moved out of this house, try just visiting.
This time the sheen of the dining table
must be one inch deep. It holds the night hours of Mother,
sanding with some silly little tool meant for dainty jobs
and dainty women, not this five foot oak circle
and the woman not much taller.

She chased the lights of the wood down grimly,
determined to have beauty,
cramped fingers covered with fine red dust.

I sit at the deep table. My brother walks in
and stops at my chair back. He outstripped me
in size and kindness years ago. He strokes my hair,
examines a hank of it with the expert eye of the woodsman.
His touch is rare; I am curious.

Your hair, he says, *is just like a beaver pelt.*
So soft and dark. With lots of red in it.

He is bent over, surprised to see such a thing here,
away from its home,
wild and shining in the house.

Multiple Injuries
(for Mark and for Wendy)

I thought of you today after I got news
of a friend who'd been hurt in a car crash,
her second one in ten years. For a year or two
after the first one, she was afraid to leave
her own house. She had to get used to
the new face the surgeon gave back to her,
practically the same as the old one.

Then yesterday, as if God weren't keeping track
of the even distribution of blows over
the general population, it happened again.
Another head injury.

It grieved me just like this to see you,
no matter how careful you were, get blamed
and hit again and again by our father
when we were small, until our little souls
moved out into the eaves of our bodies
to wait for safety.

And you still cried for me when my house burned
for the second time. For the unfairness of it,
you said, then apologized for letting yourself
break like that. But I told you then and
I tell you now, brother, those tears are a treasure.
I keep them in a cup somewhere in this newly-built house,
and today I used them to cry
for this woman wounded twice.

Then I looked out the window into the late fall
and thought I saw a moth. It had no business
being alive in this weather. But then I looked,

and in the clear air it was really a seed spinning
like mad in the wind, and I thought,
for you and for her,

I am glad for your life.

The Rooms of Older Sisters

(for Toni-Lee)

When I was just ten and you were sixteen,
you cried once, very quietly.
Trained as I was from birth to sniff out pain,
I followed up the stairs, hoping crazily
you might finally need me for something.

But you kept on climbing, up the skinny ladder
to the attic, looked at me through the rungs with the face
you wanted me to see, miserable and shut.
My stupid little sympathy wasn't welcome up there.

And as I watch my own two girls, one ten,
the other sixteen, do their own tug-of-war,
elbowing each other into and out of adulthood,
I see we're finally coming to it, too—
thirty years late, is all.

After your divorce, your children grown,
you ask me at last into your beautiful rooms.
You exclaim over my gifts to you
like a prudent queen over jewels.

And I, the tough one, the one with the foul mouth,
the one who's always taken the hard line,
I at last feel blessed. My face is the face
of my ten-year-old daughter right after her sister
has invited her up the ladder into her bed
near the ceiling for the night.
I cannot believe my good fortune.

Stopping only to sleep, we take the whole week-end.
We use forty-eight hours and thousands of words
to say over and over to each other:

Come in, sister.
This is where I've been.

Dissection at Nine Years
(for Zephyr)

Over lunch my daughter tells me that two weeks ago
she dissected sheeps' eyes in day camp.

Never mind that I pictured her slapping together
a papier mache dragon or extruding play-dough spaghettis
at the time. Never mind that I find out two whole weeks later
about this slimy initiation of my last-born.

So what did you find? I say.
We wore rubber gloves.
I nod my hygienic approval.
We cut them open with little scissors,
then we found that hard clear thing.

The lens, I say.
She tolerates my interruption blankly, politely.
The stupid word has nothing to do with the thing
she felt slipping between her fingertips,
trying to slide away whenever she squeezed.

After we found all that wet gooky stuff in the middle
and squeezed it out, we took off our gloves.

Then, she said, *we found my favorite part.*
It was all white and shiny, you know,
like that stuff mother-of-pearl.

Do you know what it was called? I say.
Nope, she says.
Just mother-of-pearl, I say.
Yup, she says.
We finally understand each other.

For days I've felt them, those two curved shells
glistening white at the backs of my eyes, accepting,
reflecting the light reflecting off things
we give names to to put them in their places.

The optic nerve, the retina,
might keep the world at bay,
but never mother-of-pearl
or girl.

Brushes

My wooden scrub brush with its waist like a woman's
is oldfangled and easy to grab.

This morning I squirted hot water into its tightly-packed bristles
and squeezed on the detergent, scrubbed horseshit
off the blue crackling tarp spread in the sun,
watched the suds work up and the dirt loosen.
Recalled the tiny brush on a handle I'd stuck into my mouth
earlier, after breakfast, to reach crevices blunt fingers can't pick.

Later, fresh from her gardening job,
my daughter rides to the bank with her paycheck,
tells me of the best brush, at her boyfriend's house,
the way it gets the dirt out from under your nails,
then decides she's proud striding into the clean bank dirty,
slapping down her money with hands that tell how it came.

Cora, Reciting
(for Cora Brooks)

One hundred of us wait for Cora
to remember the words to a poem.

She looks beyond us patiently, waiting with us
as if expecting her favorite guests.

We wait so long that we know our waiting
will help the words to come.

She smiles as she sees them rolling in.
We smile as she spills them on our feet a second later.

Her eyes are blue like that because she listens for waves
and makes them, every day, even in her sleep.

Crazy Woman Hanging Out Clothes

So here I am again hanging out clothes
as the sun goes down. I always mis-time that last laundry load
so I'm sending it out on the line into the dark.
I look like a crazy woman doing this.
People hang clothes out in the morning.
I know this.

But alone on the back porch hanging up clothes in the dark,
I reason with myself out loud:
What can happen to clothes in the dark air
that we are afraid to leave them out overnight?
Will they be gone in the morning
because we let the dark have them?
Will the dark cling to our clothes like vapors,
making us do unpredictable things when we wear them?

I decide I'm past the worrying point.
I'm standing here in the dark hanging up clothes,
talking to myself about whether hanging up clothes
in the dark is going to make me do insane things.

I look at all the things I've hung up so far, and figure
they could be made whiter than white with the light
from the stars. But why waste all that darkness?
I have a blue shirt that faded a bit
the last time it was washed. I hang it up last.
I figure it will soak up a little midnight
and be really stunning by the time the sun comes up.

Going Out

We make a place home only by walking it.
Keep putting your foot forward and down,
keep letting the ground catch you every time
you almost fall. This trust constantly moving
up through the legs can swallow even death.

After a certain age, this walking out
becomes a woman's coming back.
When she returns to the house
full as a cup, her litany may sound
dark and interior, like some bodily function:
vetch, foamflower, bladderwort.

Or she may brim over with
the latest horticultural report,
names that sound like women
getting ready to gallop off:
Purple Columbine, Black-eyed Susan, Gladiola.

No matter how strange she acts,
never worry about a woman like this,
even if she does. Her body which is her soul
needs to leave over and over.
It needs to go out from you
with eyes wide open, gathering.

And if you love the sweetness of waiting,
when you see her next, her body which is her soul
will be so full it will be too much for her
and she will invite you to drink.

New Home

I do not know this place,
this place does not know me.
I am a stranger here, pretending
to belong.

I have to introduce myself to everything I meet:
this rock, this flower, this fat moth on the cold window
trying to get in where it's warm.

I bring in the rock, the flower,
the moth wanting to be warm,
place each of them on a chair around the table,
then take the last one for myself.

The rock says, *I've waited so long for someone
to pick me up.* The primrose is a common sort,
says last fall's aphids just drove her crazy.
And the moth talks about how hard it is
to be on the outside looking in, how long it's been
since anyone commented on the pattern
of her velvet wings, how closely it mimics
some fine gray-with-gold antique Persian carpets.

I say to each of them the words we must say
to those who endure what they must. And see?
Now they are my guests and I am in my home.

About the Author

Francette Cerulli was born in New Jersey in 1949. She writes poems, essays, short stories, and a monthly column for the Barre-Montpelier *Times Argus* of Barre, Vermont. She was the recipient of *The Louisville Review*'s first-place prize for poetry, *Negative Capability*'s third-place prize for poetry for three poems, and has taught creative writing in Vermont's prisons and schools. She leads book discussions in libraries throughout the state for the Vermont Council on the Humanities. Cerulli lives in Worcester, Vermont with her husband. Together they have four children and one grandchild.

Ordering Information

To order a copy of *The Spirits Need To Eat*, please send a
check or money order for $12.95 (Vermont residents add 5%
sales tax) plus $3.00 for first-class postage and handling to:

Nine-Patch Press
579-B Minister Brook Road
Worcester, VT 05682

Bookstores and libraries, please call 802-229-9827 for dis-
count information.